HANUMAN :
THE POWER OF REALISING YOUR POTENTIAL

DR. ASHISH GUPTA

To the indomitable spirit of Hanuman,
the embodiment of devotion, courage, and boundless potential.

May his story remind us that true power lies not in mere strength but
in self-belief, devotion, and the courage to take action.

Jai Shri Ram!
Jai Hanuman!

Contents

Preface — ix

Acknowledgements — xi

Copyright — xiii

How to Use This Book — xv

About The Author — xix

Introduction: The Eternal Relevance of Hanuman's Story — xxi

Part I: The Legend Of Hanuman

The Divine Origin

1. Historical Context — 5

2. The Birth Of Hanuman And Early Life — 8

The Powers Of Hanuman

3. The Sun-Eating Incident: A Testament To His Strength — 13

4. Blessings And Curses: The Forging Of A Hero — 16

Hanuman And The Ramayana

5. Meeting With Shri Ram And Lakshman — 21

6. The Quest To Find Sita — 24

7. The Leap To Lanka — 28

Part II: The Philosophy And Symbolism Of Hanuman

Understanding Devotion And Service

8. Hanuman's Devotion To Rama — 35

9. Lessons In Selflessness And Loyalty — 39

The Strength Within

Contents

10. Realizing Inner Potential And Power   45

11. Overcoming Obstacles With Faith And   48
Perseverance

Wisdom And Humility

12. Hanuman's Intelligence And Wit   55

13. The Virtue Of Humility In Strength   59

Part III: Embodying Hanuman's Qualities In Personal Growth

Courage And Confidence

14. Facing Your Fears   67

15. Building Confidence Through Action   71

Devotion And Dedication

16. The Power Of Purpose   77

17. Living A Life Of Service And Devotion   80

Strength And Resilience

18. Cultivating Physical And Mental Strength   87

19. The Art Of Resilience In Adversity   91

Part IV: Practical Applications

Meditation And Mantras

20. Connecting With Hanuman Through Meditation   99

21. The Hanuman Chalisa: A Spiritual Tool For   103
Empowerment

Lessons From The Epic Ramayana

22. Applying Hanuman's Lessons In Modern Life   111

Contents

23. Overcoming Personal Challenges With Grace And Strength — 115

Community And Belief

24. The Importance Of Community In Spiritual Growth — 121

25. Fostering Belief And Faith In Oneself — 125

Part V: Epilogue

26. Reflecting On The Journey — 131

27. Hanuman: A Beacon Of Hope And Strength — 134

Major Characters in the Ramayana — 137

References and Further Reading — 141

Preface

Welcome to a journey through the life and teachings of Hanuman, an embodiment of devotion, strength, and selflessness. This exploration is not just a recounting of ancient tales but a passage to understanding how Hanuman's virtues are more than mythological ideals; they are practical guides for navigating the complexities of modern life.

Hanuman's story, woven into the fabric of the epic Ramayana, has captivated the hearts and minds of millions for centuries. Yet, the lessons it holds are not bound by time or culture. They speak to the universal quest for meaning, the struggle against adversities, and the pursuit of righteousness amidst life's trials. This book aims to bridge the ancient wisdom embodied by Hanuman with the challenges of contemporary living, offering insights into cultivating resilience, integrity, and compassion in our daily lives.

Why Hanuman? Among the pantheon of deities and heroes in Hindu history, Hanuman stands out for his unwavering commitment to dharma (righteous duty), his extraordinary feats achieved through faith and devotion, and his humility despite immense power. These qualities make Hanuman a timeless exemplar of character and virtue, offering a beacon of inspiration for all who seek to live a life of purpose and devotion.

As we delve into Hanuman's adventures, from his birth to his pivotal role in the victory of good over evil, we uncover the layers of symbolism and teaching that his story offers. Each chapter of this book is designed to reflect on different aspects of Hanuman's character — his courage, loyalty, intelligence, and selflessness and how these can inform our personal development and spiritual growth.

This book is for anyone on a journey of self-improvement and spiritual inquiry. Whether you are well-acquainted with Hanuman's story or encountering it for the first time, there is a wealth of wisdom to be discovered. Through reflections, anecdotes, and analyses, we invite you to draw upon Hanuman's example to face life's challenges with grace and strength, to deepen your faith, and to cultivate a spirit of service and humility.

Let the journey begin.

Acknowledgements

My reverence and thanks go to the ancient sages and poets, especially Sage Valmiki and Saint Tulsidas, whose epic works have preserved Hanuman's legacy through the ages. Their timeless compositions have not only served as the foundation for this exploration but have also been a source of light and guidance in moments of doubt and reflection.

Jai Hanuman

Copyright

How To Use This Book

Embarking on a journey through this book, inspired by the life and teachings of Hanuman, offers a unique opportunity for personal growth, spiritual understanding, and the cultivation of virtues that can transform our lives. To maximize the benefits of this exploration, here are some guidelines on how to use this book effectively:

1. Approach with Openness and Curiosity: Begin your journey with an open heart and mind, ready to explore the depths of Hanuman's teachings. Allow curiosity to guide your engagement with the text, encouraging a deeper understanding of the lessons and how they apply to modern life.

2. Reflective Reading: Instead of rushing through the chapters, take your time to read reflectively. Pause at moments that resonate with you or challenge your perceptions. Reflect on how Hanuman's qualities of devotion, strength, humility, and wisdom can be integrated into your own life.

3. Journaling: Keep a journal handy as you read. Writing down your thoughts, insights, and reflections can enhance your understanding and retention of the lessons. Journaling can also serve as a personal space for exploring how Hanuman's journey mirrors your own challenges and aspirations.

4. Practical Application: Each chapter is designed not only to offer insights into Hanuman's life but also to suggest practical applications of these lessons in daily life. Look for these actionable steps and consider how you can implement them to cultivate strength, resilience, devotion, and humility.

5. Discussion and Community Engagement: Share your insights and reflections with others. Discussing the book's content with friends, family, or in a study group can enrich your understanding and offer diverse perspectives on Hanuman's teachings. Engaging with a community can also mirror Hanuman's emphasis on service, teamwork, and collective growth.

6. Meditation and Contemplation: Dedicate time for meditation or contemplation on the qualities of Hanuman that most inspire you. Whether it's his unwavering devotion, incredible strength, profound humility, or keen intellect, meditating on these virtues can facilitate a deeper internalization and personal transformation.

7. Revisiting the Text: This book is meant to be a companion on your journey, offering guidance and inspiration as you navigate life's challenges. Feel free to revisit chapters or sections that speak to you at different times, as the lessons may reveal new meanings and insights as your own journey unfolds.

8. Integration into Daily Life: Look for opportunities to integrate the virtues and teachings of Hanuman into your daily life. Whether it's through acts of kindness, moments of reflection, overcoming personal challenges, or deepening your spiritual practices, find ways to embody the lessons learned.

By engaging with this book in these ways, you embark on a transformative journey that transcends mere intellectual understanding, moving towards a heartfelt integration of Hanuman's timeless virtues into the fabric of your daily life. May this exploration inspire you to face life with greater courage, devotion, and humility, guided by the light of Hanuman's example.

About The Author

Dr. Ashish Gupta is a dynamic thought leader, career coach, and author dedicated to helping individuals realize their full potential. With over 14 years of expertise in the education sector, he has been a driving force in inspiring students, professionals, and entrepreneurs to unlock their unique capabilities and achieve meaningful success. Ashish is on a mission to empower India's youth and workforce to excel in an ever-changing world.

Blending ancient Indian wisdom with modern strategies, Ashish focuses on leadership, personal growth, ethics, and skill development to create practical frameworks for success. Known for his ability to simplify profound ideas, he delivers actionable insights that resonate with people across diverse backgrounds. His work emphasizes the power of consistent effort, purposeful action, and self-belief as the cornerstones of a fulfilling life.

Ashish believes that success is not just a destination but a journey of dreaming boldly and taking small, consistent steps every day. Through his books, coaching sessions, and public speaking engagements, he continues to motivate others to break barriers, harness their potential, and lead extraordinary lives.

When he isn't writing or coaching, Ashish explores India's rich cultural heritage, mentors aspiring professionals, and contributes to initiatives aimed at building a prosperous and developed nation.

To connect with Ashish Gupta and explore more about his work, visit ashishgupta.co.in, follow him on Linkedin at https://www.linkedin.com/in/theashishgupta/ or write to him at authorashishgupta@gmail.com

Introduction: The Eternal Relevance Of Hanuman's Story

The story of Hanuman, an emblematic figure in Hindu history, transcends the confines of time and geography, resonating with universal themes of devotion, strength, and the pursuit of righteousness. As the central figure in many ancient Indian epics, most notably the Ramayana, Hanuman's narrative is not just a series of historical events but a profound exposition on the depth of spiritual discipline, unwavering faith, and the power of realizing one's innate potential. This introduction seeks to illuminate the eternal relevance of Hanuman's story, exploring how his journey from a deity to a symbol of ultimate devotion and strength offers profound insights into the human condition and the path to personal growth and enlightenment.

Hanuman's tale is a vibrant tapestry of adventure, heroism, and divine play, marked by his extraordinary feats, deep humility, and boundless devotion to Lord Rama. Beyond the surface of these legendary exploits lies a rich vein of spiritual and philosophical teachings relevant to anyone seeking to navigate the complexities of life with grace, courage, and a sense of purpose. Hanuman embodies the potential within us to transcend our limitations, reminding us that with faith, devotion, and perseverance, we can achieve the seemingly impossible.

In a world that often prizes material success and external achievements, Hanuman's story offers a counter-narrative that valorizes inner strength, selflessness, and the pursuit of spiritual goals. His devotion to Rama is not just a tale of divine service but a metaphor for the dedication required to realize one's own divinity and potential. Hanuman's journey teaches us that true strength lies in character, integrity, and the unwavering conviction to stand by one's principles and loved ones, even in the face of daunting challenges.

Furthermore, Hanuman's wisdom and humility, despite his immense powers, serve as a guiding light for personal development. They teach us the importance of recognizing our own abilities and using them for the greater good, rather than personal gain. In an age where ego and individualism often dominate, Hanuman's story is a powerful reminder of the virtues of humility, service, and community.

This book aims to explore the layers of meaning within Hanuman's story, drawing out lessons that are as relevant today as they were centuries ago. Through an examination of his character, deeds, and the symbolism embedded in his narrative, we will delve into how Hanuman's journey can inspire us to realize our potential, face our lives' challenges with courage, and ultimately, find our path to spiritual and personal fulfillment.

In the pages that follow, I invite you to journey with us through the life of Hanuman, discovering along the way how his timeless story can illuminate the path to realizing your potential, fostering resilience, and living a life of purpose and devotion. Hanuman's legacy, rich with lessons on power, devotion, and enlightenment, offers each of us a mirror to our souls and a beacon of hope in our quest for personal growth and spiritual awakening.

Part I: The Legend of Hanuman

The Divine Origin

CHAPTER ONE

Historical Context

To fully appreciate the significance of Hanuman and the profound messages embedded in his story, it's essential to delve into the Historical context in which his tale unfolds. Hanuman is a pivotal figure in Hindu history, prominently featured in epic narratives such as the Ramayana and, to a lesser extent, the Mahabharata. Understanding this context not only illuminates Hanuman's character and deeds but also enriches our interpretation of the spiritual and moral lessons his story conveys.

The Tapestry of Hindu History

Hindu history is a vast and intricate tapestry of stories, gods, and cosmic principles that form the backbone of Hindu spiritual and cultural beliefs. It encompasses a wide array of deities, each embodying different aspects of the divine and the human experience. Within this rich mosaic, Hanuman stands out as a symbol of devotion, strength, and righteousness. His adventures are set against the backdrop of the Ramayana, an ancient epic that narrates the life of Lord Rama, an avatar of Vishnu, and his quest to rescue his wife Sita from the demon king Ravana.

The Ramayana: A Foundational Epic

The Ramayana, attributed to the sage Valmiki, is not just a story of adventure and conflict; it's a deeply spiritual and moral text that has shaped the ethical and cultural fabric of many societies. It teaches the values of duty (dharma), devotion (bhakti), and the importance of righteousness. Hanuman's role in this epic is central, serving as a bridge between the divine and the human, demonstrating the power of faith and the potential within each individual to contribute to the greater good.

Hanuman's Divine Heritage

Hanuman is unique among the deities in Hindu history. Born to Anjana, and Kesari, a vanara (monkey) chief, with the wind god, Vayu, as his divine patron, Hanuman is at once a figure of divine descent and a being closely connected to the earthly realm. This dual heritage underscores his role as a mediator between the human and divine worlds, capable of extraordinary feats yet always grounded in his devotion to Rama and the principles of dharma.

Symbolism and Significance

Hanuman's story is replete with symbolic elements that reflect deeper spiritual truths. His very name, derived from 'Hanu' (jaw) and 'man' (prominent), references the legend of his jaw being broken by Indra's thunderbolt in his childhood, symbolizing the trials and transformations that precede spiritual awakening. His ability to change size at will represents the yogic mastery over the physical form, and his leap across the Indian Ocean to Lanka symbolizes the power of faith to overcome daunting obstacles.

A Figure of Devotion and Courage

Above all, Hanuman embodies the ideal devotee. His unwavering dedication to Rama, even in the face of severe trials, exemplifies the path of bhakti (devotion) as a means to divine connection and spiritual liberation. His courage, intelligence, and humility serve as models for human conduct, emphasizing the importance of selflessness, service, and devotion in the pursuit of spiritual and worldly objectives.

Understanding the Historical context of Hanuman's story enriches our appreciation of his significance within Hindu history and offers timeless lessons on the power of devotion, the strength within, and the importance of living a life aligned with dharma. Hanuman's journey from myth to symbol of ultimate faith and strength continues to inspire individuals across generations, reminding us of the potential within each of us to rise to our highest capabilities.

CHAPTER TWO

The Birth of Hanuman and Early Life

Hanuman's story begins with divine intervention and celestial foretelling, setting the stage for his extraordinary life as a figure of immense power, unwavering devotion, and unparalleled service. His origins are a testament to the intricate interplay between the divine and the terrestrial in Hindu mythology, offering a glimpse into the deep symbolism and spiritual significance that his life embodies.

The Birth of Hanuman

The birth of Hanuman is a narrative rich in divine orchestration, rooted in ancient texts and traditions. Anjana, a celestial nymph (apsara) who was transformed into a monkey due to a curse, and Kesari, a valiant monkey chief, prayed fervently to Lord Shiva for a child. Moved by their devotion, Shiva granted them a son, who would be his avatar, embodying his strength, courage, and wisdom.

The wind god, Vayu, played a crucial role in Hanuman's birth, carrying the divine prasad (blessed offering) from Lord Shiva to Anjana, ensuring that Hanuman would be born with divine qualities. This divine heritage bestowed upon Hanuman remarkable abilities and a destiny intertwined with the divine play of the gods.

Early Life and Divine Play

From his earliest days, Hanuman exhibited signs of his extraordinary nature. One famous legend recounts his insatiable hunger as a child, mistaking the sun for a ripe fruit and attempting to leap up and swallow it. This act of audacity brought him into conflict with Indra, the king of gods, who struck him with his thunderbolt, Vajra, injuring Hanuman's jaw (hanu). This incident earned him the name Hanuman and highlighted his fearless spirit and boundless potential.

Vayu, angered by the injury to his surrogate son, withdrew the air from the world, threatening all life. The gods, recognizing Hanuman's divine nature and fearing the consequences of Vayu's wrath, conferred upon Hanuman multiple boons: Indra granted him immunity from his thunderbolt; Agni, the fire god, made him immune to fire; Surya, the sun god, bestowed upon him immense knowledge and brilliance; and Brahma, the creator, promised that no weapon could harm him. These boons not only healed Hanuman but also made him invincible, marking him as a being of divine significance.

Education and Acquiring Powers

Hanuman's education was as remarkable as his birth. He studied under the sun god, Surya, acquiring knowledge in various scriptures, languages, and the art of warfare. Surya recognized Hanuman's exceptional qualities but asked for no guru dakshina (teacher's fee), as there was nothing Hanuman could offer that Surya did not already possess. Instead, Hanuman's service to Surya's son, Sugriva, was considered an adequate exchange, setting the stage for Hanuman's role in the events of the Ramayana.

Symbolism and Lessons

Hanuman's divine origins and early exploits symbolize the latent potential within all beings to rise above their nature and achieve greatness. His story teaches us about the power of devotion, the importance of humility, and the strength that comes from selfless service. Hanuman's life, from its miraculous beginning to his deeds in service of Lord Rama, serves as an enduring symbol of the possibility of transcending limitations through faith, devotion, and the blessings of the divine.

As we delve further into Hanuman's adventures and his indispensable role in the epic saga of the Ramayana, we continue to uncover layers of meaning and relevance that his story holds for understanding the essence of devotion, strength, and the realization of one's potential.

The Powers of Hanuman

The Sun-Eating Incident: A Testament to His Strength

The sun-eating incident in Hanuman's early life is not just a testament to his extraordinary strength but also a profound symbol of his boundless potential and fearless spirit. This event, occurring when Hanuman was but a child, encapsulates the themes of divine intervention, the interplay of cosmic forces, and the latent capabilities within us that await realization.

The Incident

The tale begins with young Hanuman, imbued with insatiable curiosity and unmatched vitality, gazing upon the rising sun. Mistaking it for a ripe, glowing fruit, he was overcome with the desire to reach out and consume it. Such was the strength and determination of Hanuman that he took a mighty leap towards the sun, traversing the vast sky with the intention of swallowing it whole. This act of incredible audacity and innocence set the stage for a dramatic confrontation with the celestial order.

The Divine Response

The gods, witnessing this unprecedented event, were taken aback by Hanuman's powers. The sun god, Surya, appealed to Indra, the king of gods, to intervene and prevent Hanuman from swallowing the sun, which would plunge the world into darkness and chaos. Indra, in an attempt to stop Hanuman, unleashed his thunderbolt (Vajra), striking Hanuman and causing him to fall back down to the earth. The impact injured Hanuman's jaw (hanu), a wound that led to his name, Hanuman, but also signaled the divine acknowledgment of his extraordinary nature.

The Boons Conferred

The fallout from this incident was significant. Vayu, the wind god and Hanuman's divine patron, in response to the injury inflicted upon Hanuman, withdrew his essence from the world, leading to a catastrophic absence of air. Life on earth began to suffocate, compelling the gods to convene and deliberate on a solution. Recognizing the gravity of their actions and the potential within Hanuman, the gods collectively decided to bestow upon him a series of boons. These boons not only healed him but also rendered him invulnerable to similar assaults in the future, marking him as a divine entity with a special role to play in the cosmic order.

Symbolism and Lessons

The sun-eating incident is rich in symbolic meaning. It

highlights the theme of youthful innocence and the exploration of one's potential without the constraints of fear or hesitation. Hanuman's leap towards the sun represents the soul's yearning for knowledge and the pursuit of the divine light, signifying the boundless aspirations that drive us towards self-realization and spiritual growth.

Moreover, the incident underscores the importance of divine grace and the protective powers of the universe that guide and shape our destinies. The boons conferred upon Hanuman by the gods symbolize the rewards of courage, resilience, and faith, illustrating how trials and tribulations can lead to empowerment and blessings.

Enduring Relevance

The story of Hanuman's sun-eating incident continues to inspire, serving as a metaphor for the human potential to achieve greatness despite seemingly insurmountable challenges. It teaches us the value of daring to reach beyond our perceived limits, embracing our innate strengths, and trusting in the divine support that sustains us through our journeys. Hanuman's tale, starting from this pivotal moment, is a reminder that within each of us lies the capability to transcend ordinary existence and touch the essence of the divine.

CHAPTER FOUR

Blessings and Curses: The Forging of a Hero

Hanuman's journey from a divine child with immense potential to a hero of epic proportions is intricately laced with a series of blessings and curses that shaped his destiny. These events, far from being mere episodes of divine whim, serve as pivotal moments in Hanuman's life, each carrying profound lessons on the interplay of fate, free will, and the path to self-realization. They underscore the dual nature of life's experiences, illustrating how adversities and blessings are instrumental in the forging of a hero.

The Curse of Forgetfulness

One of the most significant turning points in Hanuman's life was the curse of forgetfulness bestowed upon him during his childhood. Following the sun-eating incident, and as Hanuman continued to display his boundless energy and strength in ways that sometimes alarmed the sages and hermits, one such sage, angered by Hanuman's mischievous disturbances, cursed him to forget his divine powers. This curse was not lifted until much later in his life, at a crucial moment when his powers were needed the most.

The curse symbolizes the periods of dormancy and potential that lie within each individual, waiting to be awakened at the right moment. It speaks to the journey of self-discovery, where the true extent of one's abilities is often realized in the face of adversity.

The Blessing of Immortality

In contrast to the curse, Hanuman was also the recipient of numerous blessings that augmented his divine nature and capabilities. Among these was the blessing of immortality, conferred upon him for his unwavering devotion and service to Lord Rama. This boon not only signifies Hanuman's eternal role in the cosmic play but also represents the immortal nature of devotion and righteousness that transcends the physical bounds of life and death.

The Power of Remembrance

The moment of Hanuman's awakening to his forgotten powers is a key episode in the Ramayana, occurring when he is reminded of his abilities during the search for Sita. This awakening is facilitated by Jambavan, the king of bears, who helps Hanuman remember his divine capabilities. This act of remembrance serves as a catalyst for Hanuman's monumental leap across the ocean to Lanka, marking the beginning of his pivotal role in the events of the Ramayana.

This moment underscores the importance of guidance and mentorship in unlocking one's potential. It highlights how, often, the key to overcoming obstacles lies within us, awaiting the right trigger to unleash our innate strengths.

The Role of Curses and Blessings in Shaping Destiny

The interplay of curses and blessings in Hanuman's life illustrates a deeper philosophical truth: that our journey is shaped by a combination of challenges and support, each playing a crucial role in our development. The curses Hanuman faced prepared him by instilling humility and patience, while the blessings he received were a recognition of his devotion, courage, and the purity of his heart.

Enduring Lessons

Hanuman's story teaches us that adversity and support are not opposites but complementary forces that drive personal growth and transformation. The curses that led to periods of forgetfulness and the blessings that bestowed upon him divine gifts both contributed to Hanuman's evolution into a hero of epic stature. His journey from oblivion to omnipotence, from cursed forgetfulness to the pinnacle of divine achievement, embodies the potential for transformation that lies within each of us.

Through the lens of Hanuman's life, we are reminded that our greatest trials can lead to our most profound revelations, and that within every curse lies the seed of a blessing, waiting to be realized. Hanuman's story, thus, is not just the tale of a divine hero but a guide for navigating the dualities of life, embracing our challenges, and unlocking the hero within.

Hanuman and the Ramayana

CHAPTER FIVE

Meeting with Shri Ram and Lakshman

The meeting of Hanuman with Shri Ram and Lakshmana is a pivotal moment in the epic Ramayana, marking the beginning of a divine friendship and an unbreakable bond of devotion, loyalty, and brotherhood. This event not only signifies a turning point in the narrative but also embodies deep spiritual and philosophical teachings about destiny, divine connections, and the power of true devotion.

The Background

Rama, the prince of Ayodhya and the seventh avatar of Lord Vishnu, along with his brother Lakshmana, was in search of his wife, Sita, who had been abducted by the demon king Ravana. Their quest led them to the forests of Kishkindha, the realm of the vanaras (monkey kingdom), where fate was set to orchestrate the momentous meeting.

The First Encounter

Hanuman, serving under the vanara king Sugriva, was the first to spot Rama and Lakshmana as they neared

Kishkindha. Sugriva, wary of potential threats, dispatched Hanuman to ascertain the strangers' intentions. Disguising himself as a brahmin, Hanuman approached the brothers with a blend of curiosity and caution. His initial encounter with Rama and Lakshmana is marked by profound respect and an intuitive recognition of Rama's divinity, despite his human guise.

The Revelation and Alliance

Upon meeting Rama, Hanuman realizes the divine nature of his mission and reveals his true form. He narrates Sugriva's tale of woe — his wrongful exile by his brother Vali — and expresses Sugriva's desire for friendship and alliance with Rama. This moment is crucial, for it sets the stage for the coalition between Rama and the vanaras, a union pivotal to the success of Rama's quest.

The conversation between Rama and Hanuman is rich with spiritual and emotional depth, highlighting Hanuman's eloquence, wisdom, and devotion. Rama is deeply moved by Hanuman's sincerity and intelligence, remarking that his words are like soothing balm to his sorrows. This exchange marks the beginning of Hanuman's unwavering devotion to Rama, setting the foundation for all his future endeavors in service of Rama and Sita.

Symbolism and Teachings

The meeting between Hanuman, Rama, and Lakshmana symbolizes the divine orchestration of relationships that are destined to unfold in our lives, serving larger cosmic purposes. It underscores the importance of dharma (righteousness) and bhakti (devotion) in the path to divine realization and the fulfillment of one's life missions.

Hanuman's initial disguise and subsequent revelation to Rama teach us the value of discernment and the recognition of divinity in all beings. Furthermore, this event highlights the theme of divine assistance — how, in our moments of greatest need, the universe conspires to bring us together with those who can help us fulfill our destiny.

The Impact of the Meeting

The alliance formed as a result of this meeting is instrumental in the search for Sita and the eventual defeat of Ravana. Hanuman's role as a messenger, warrior, and devoted servant of Rama begins here, embodying the ideal of selfless service and devotion. This meeting is celebrated in various texts and traditions as a moment of divine connection, illustrating how faith, devotion, and righteousness bring together forces capable of overcoming great adversities.

In the broader spiritual narrative, the encounter between Hanuman, Rama, and Lakshmana teaches us about the power of divine will, the importance of noble companionships on our spiritual journey, and the transformative power of devotion. Hanuman's unwavering dedication to Rama, sparked by this initial meeting, continues to inspire devotion and loyalty across generations, highlighting the eternal relevance of their story in the pursuit of truth, righteousness, and divine love.

CHAPTER SIX

The Quest to Find Sita

The quest to find Sita is a central narrative arc in the Ramayana, illustrating themes of loyalty, perseverance, and the power of teamwork in the face of daunting challenges. This quest not only underscores the epic's emotional depth but also highlights Hanuman's indispensable role in the search for Rama's abducted wife, showcasing his bravery, intelligence, and unwavering devotion.

The Formation of the Search Party

Following the alliance between Rama and Sugriva, the vanara king, a massive search operation was organized to find Sita. Sugriva dispatched thousands of vanaras (monkey warriors) in all directions across the Indian subcontinent, with specific search parties assigned to explore various regions. Hanuman was part of the team directed towards the south, where the chances of finding Sita were most promising, given the clues available.

The Challenges of the Quest

The search for Sita was fraught with obstacles and challenges. The vastness of the terrain, the uncertainty of

Sita's whereabouts, and the myriad dangers lurking in unknown lands tested the resolve and strength of Rama's allies. The vanaras searched mountains, forests, and valleys, facing not just physical exhaustion but also the emotional toll of a seemingly endless search.

The Leap of Faith

The turning point in the quest came when the search party reached the southern shore of India, facing the vast expanse of the ocean that lay between them and Lanka, where Sita was believed to be held captive. With the realization that crossing the ocean was the next insurmountable challenge, it was Hanuman who emerged as the beacon of hope.

Reminded of his forgotten divine powers by Jambavan, Hanuman took a monumental leap of faith from the shores of India to the island of Lanka. This leap was not just a physical feat but a symbol of overcoming the impossible through faith, determination, and devotion. It epitomizes the strength that lies in belief — in oneself and in the divine.

Hanuman's Adventures in Lanka

Upon reaching Lanka, Hanuman embarked on a covert mission to find Sita. His adventures in the enemy territory are marked by cunning, bravery, and the singular focus on his mission. Hanuman's search led him to Ashoka Vatika, where he finally found Sita, imprisoned and in sorrow. The meeting between Hanuman and Sita is a poignant moment in the Ramayana, symbolizing hope and the assurance of salvation.

Hanuman not only confirmed Sita's whereabouts but also conveyed Rama's message of love and promised liberation. Before leaving Lanka, he caused significant damage to the demon king Ravana's kingdom, signaling the inevitable war and the strength of Rama's resolve to rescue his beloved wife.

The Return and the Preparation for War

Hanuman's return to Rama, bearing the news of Sita's location and the state of affairs in Lanka, was a moment of mixed emotions — joy at the success of the quest and the anticipation of the challenges that lay ahead in the battle against Ravana. His successful mission galvanized Rama and his allies, setting the stage for the epic battle to come.

Symbolic and Philosophical Significance

The quest to find Sita, particularly Hanuman's role in it, teaches profound lessons on devotion, the strength of will, and the power of faith to transcend obstacles. Hanuman's journey is a metaphor for the soul's search for the divine, illustrating how devotion and perseverance lead to the ultimate realization of one's goals. It also highlights the importance of teamwork and collective effort in overcoming life's challenges, with each individual's unique strengths contributing to the achievement of a common goal.

In essence, the quest to find Sita underscores the enduring values of loyalty, courage, and the unshakeable belief in righteousness, with Hanuman's contributions epitomizing the pinnacle of devotion and selfless service.

CHAPTER SEVEN

The Leap to Lanka

The leap to Lanka stands as one of the most iconic and spiritually significant episodes in the Ramayana, epitomizing Hanuman's unwavering faith, boundless courage, and the power of devotion. This monumental act not only demonstrated Hanuman's extraordinary abilities but also his profound dedication to Lord Rama and the mission to rescue Sita. It serves as a vivid illustration of overcoming seemingly insurmountable obstacles through belief in oneself and divine support.

The Moment of Determination

Faced with the vast expanse of the ocean that separated the search party from Lanka, where Sita was held captive, the task of finding her seemed nearly impossible. The morale of the search team was waning, with the daunting realization that none possessed the power to leap across the ocean. It was at this critical juncture that Jambavan, the wise bear, reminded Hanuman of his forgotten divine powers, instilling in him the confidence to undertake the mission.

The Preparation for the Leap

Inspired and rejuvenated by the reminder of his latent capabilities, Hanuman grew in size and strength, embodying the very essence of his divine heritage. Standing on Mount Mahendra, he focused his mind, chanted Rama's name, and with determination in his heart, made the colossal leap towards Lanka. This moment is celebrated for its dramatic portrayal of faith and the visualization of Hanuman's devotion, as he surmounted the physical distance between him and his divine purpose.

The Journey Across the Ocean

Hanuman's journey across the ocean was fraught with challenges. He encountered several obstacles, including a demonic sea creature that sought to devour him and a mountain that rose from the sea offering him rest. Yet, Hanuman, driven by his devotion to Rama and the urgency of his mission, overcame these challenges with wisdom, strength, and the invocation of Rama's name. These encounters during his leap symbolize the trials and temptations that devotees face on their spiritual path, demonstrating the power of faith to overcome them.

The Significance of the Leap

The leap to Lanka is not just a testament to Hanuman's physical prowess but a deeper allegory for the spiritual leap of faith. It represents the journey of the soul towards the divine, overcoming the ocean of existence and ignorance to reach the goal of divine love and liberation. Hanuman's unwavering focus on Rama throughout the leap embodies the essence of Bhakti Yoga, the path of devotion, where the devotee transcends the physical bounds of the world through unwavering love and dedication to God.

The Impact of Hanuman's Arrival in Lanka

Upon reaching Lanka, Hanuman's mission took a crucial turn as he went on to locate Sita, reassure her of Rama's efforts to rescue her, and assess the strength of Ravana's forces. His actions in Lanka, including the burning of Lanka to demonstrate the power of Rama's allies, set the stage for the eventual battle and Sita's rescue. Hanuman's leap, therefore, was not just a physical journey but a pivotal event that bridged the initial search with the climax of the epic battle, underscoring his role as the messenger of hope and the embodiment of fearless devotion.

Reflection

The leap to Lanka, rich in symbolism and spiritual depth, continues to inspire as a story of faith, courage, and the victory of devotion over despair. It teaches that no matter how insurmountable the obstacles in our path may seem, armed with faith in the divine and in our inner strength, we can achieve the extraordinary. Hanuman's leap is a reminder of the power of devotion to propel us forward, transcending the limitations of the mundane to embrace the possibilities of the divine.

Part II: The Philosophy and Symbolism of Hanuman

Understanding Devotion and Service

CHAPTER EIGHT

Hanuman's Devotion to Rama

Hanuman's devotion to Rama is a cornerstone of the Ramayana, symbolizing the pinnacle of unwavering faith, selfless service, and pure love. This devotion is not only central to understanding Hanuman's character but also offers profound insights into the nature of Bhakti (devotion) and its transformative power in spiritual practice. Hanuman's relationship with Rama transcends that of a servant and deity; it is a deep, personal bond that exemplifies the ideal of devotion in Hindu philosophy.

The Nature of Hanuman's Devotion

Hanuman's devotion to Rama is characterized by its selflessness and purity. Unlike other devotees who might seek blessings or favors in return, Hanuman serves Rama with no thought for his own gain. His actions, motivated solely by the love and adoration of Rama, embody the essence of Nishkama Bhakti (selfless devotion). This form of devotion is marked by a total surrender to the will of the deity, where the devotee's only desire is to serve and please the divine.

Manifestations of His Devotion

Hanuman's devotion to Rama is manifested through his deeds throughout the Ramayana:

1. The Search for Sita: Hanuman's leap to Lanka to search for Sita, braving dangers and overcoming obstacles, is driven by his devotion to Rama. His determination to succeed, fueled by his faith in Rama, showcases the extent to which he is willing to go in his service.

2. Confrontation with Ravana: In Lanka, Hanuman confronts Ravana, delivering Rama's message and advocating for Sita's release. His fearless stance against Ravana, despite the potential consequences, illustrates his unwavering commitment to Rama's cause.

3. The Sanjeevani Mountain: When Lakshmana is critically injured in the battle against Ravana, Hanuman lifts and brings the entire Dronagiri mountain to ensure Lakshmana receives the life-saving herb. This act of incredible strength and determination further highlights his devotion to Rama and his readiness to do anything for Rama's well-being.

4. Rama's Ring: Before leaping to Lanka, Rama gives Hanuman his ring as a token for Sita. Hanuman's acceptance of the ring, and his emotional reaction to receiving something so intimately connected to Rama, reflect the deep, personal bond he shares with Rama.

5. Refusal of Rewards: After the battle, when Rama offers rewards to everyone, Hanuman seeks no material possession or boon but the continuation of his service to Rama, which he considers the highest reward. His refusal of any reward other than the joy of serving Rama exemplifies the highest form of devotion.

The Impact of His Devotion

Hanuman's devotion impacts not only the course of events in the Ramayana but also the spiritual understanding of devotion itself. His actions provide a tangible expression of Bhakti, demonstrating how devotion can lead to divine grace and the fulfillment of spiritual and worldly duties. Hanuman becomes a model for devotees, illustrating that through sincere devotion, one can achieve both personal salvation and the power to assist others in their spiritual journey.

Philosophical Significance

In Hindu philosophy, Hanuman's devotion is seen as an ideal form of Bhakti. It teaches that true devotion is characterized by selflessness, purity, and the surrender of the ego to the divine will. Hanuman's relationship with Rama transcends the physical realm, entering a spiritual dimension where love and devotion are both the means and the end of the spiritual quest.

In summary, Hanuman's devotion to Rama is a profound narrative of love, faith, and sacrifice. It serves as a guiding light for the path of devotion, showing that through unwavering faith and selfless service, one can achieve the highest spiritual fulfillment and closeness to the divine.

Hanuman's devotion is not just a testament to his greatness but a reflection of the boundless potential of devotion to transform and elevate the soul.

CHAPTER NINE

Lessons in Selflessness and Loyalty

Hanuman's life, deeply intertwined with his unwavering devotion to Lord Rama, is a rich source of lessons in selflessness and loyalty. These virtues, exemplified through Hanuman's actions and character, offer timeless guidance for cultivating a life of purpose, dedication, and spiritual fulfillment. Let's explore some key lessons drawn from Hanuman's embodiment of selflessness and loyalty.

Selflessness: Putting Others Before Self

1. Joy in Service: Hanuman's actions are driven by the joy of serving Lord Rama, without any desire for recognition or reward. This teaches us the value of finding fulfillment in the act of service itself, rather than in external accolades or rewards. Serving others with a genuine heart can lead to profound personal satisfaction and joy.

2. Empathy and Compassion: Hanuman's endeavors, especially in his search for Sita, are marked by deep empathy and compassion. He demonstrates how putting oneself in another's shoes and acting from a place of understanding and kindness is a powerful form of selflessness. This empathy guides us to act thoughtfully and help those in need, reflecting a profound understanding of others' suffering.

3. Sacrifice and Dedication: The lengths to which Hanuman goes to serve Lord Rama, such as his leap to Lanka, highlight the essence of sacrifice and dedication. True selflessness often involves personal sacrifice and a commitment to a cause greater than oneself. Hanuman teaches that true growth and fulfillment come from dedicating oneself to something beyond personal interests.

Loyalty: Unwavering Commitment

1. Faithfulness in Adversity: Hanuman's loyalty to Rama never wavers, even in the face of daunting challenges. His unwavering commitment, even when the odds are against him, teaches the importance of steadfastness in our convictions and relationships, especially during difficult times.

2. Integrity and Honesty: Hanuman's interactions, characterized by honesty and transparency, underscore the importance of integrity in loyalty. True loyalty involves being truthful and sincere, qualities that strengthen bonds and build trust.

3. Protecting and Upholding Honor: Hanuman not only protects Sita but also upholds her honor, demonstrating loyalty not just in allegiance but in protecting and respecting the dignity of those we are loyal to. Loyalty involves standing up for others, defending their honor, and ensuring their well-being.

Integrating Lessons into Daily Life

1. Service as a Way of Life: Embrace opportunities for service in daily interactions and responsibilities. Acts of kindness and help, no matter how small, can make a significant difference in others' lives.

2. Empathy in Communication: Practice empathy by actively listening to others, trying to understand their perspectives, and responding with compassion and kindness.

3. Commitment to Relationships: Cultivate loyalty in relationships through consistency, reliability, and open communication. Show up for people, not just in easy times but especially in moments of hardship.

4. Personal Integrity: Live with honesty and integrity, ensuring that your actions align with your values. This builds self-respect and trust with others.

5. Advocacy and Defense: Stand up for those who cannot defend themselves. Protecting others' rights and dignity is a profound act of loyalty.

Hanuman's life is a blueprint for living with selflessness and loyalty, virtues that enrich our lives and the lives of those around us. By embodying these qualities, we can navigate life's challenges with grace and purpose, contributing to a more compassionate and understanding world.

The Strength Within

CHAPTER TEN

Realizing Inner Potential and Power

Hanuman's story, particularly the moment when he realizes his immense capabilities while preparing to leap across the ocean, serves as a powerful allegory for the realization of one's inner potential and power. This episode and Hanuman's character overall offer profound insights into unlocking the latent strengths within us. Let's explore how Hanuman's journey can inspire us to discover and harness our own inner potential.

Understanding Your Inner Potential

1. **Self-Discovery Through Challenges:** Hanuman's realization of his powers came at a moment of great need. Similarly, our own potential often becomes apparent when we face challenges. Embracing difficulties as opportunities for growth can lead to significant self-discoveries and the realization of our capabilities.

2. **The Role of Mentorship and Encouragement:** Just as Jambavan reminded Hanuman of his forgotten powers, mentors can play a crucial role in our lives by recognizing

and encouraging our potential. Seek out mentors who believe in you and listen when they reflect your strengths back to you, even when you might not see them yourself.

3. Faith and Belief in Oneself: Hanuman's leap was fueled by his faith in Rama and belief in the purpose of his mission. Similarly, having faith in our abilities and the value of our endeavors is crucial. Cultivate a positive belief system that supports your capability to overcome obstacles and achieve your goals.

Unlocking and Harnessing Your Power

1. Meditation and Mindfulness: Hanuman's focus and concentration before the leap demonstrate the power of mental preparation. Practicing meditation and mindfulness can help clear self-doubt, allowing us to tap into our inner strength and intuition.

2. Physical and Mental Discipline: Hanuman's physical prowess was matched by his mental discipline. Incorporating regular physical activity and challenging ourselves mentally can enhance our resilience, making us better prepared to face life's challenges.

3. Embracing Versatility and Adaptability: Hanuman demonstrated a remarkable ability to adapt, whether it was changing his size or finding innovative solutions to problems. Cultivating flexibility in thinking and being open to learning new skills can unlock new avenues for realizing our potential.

Applying Your Potential for the Greater Good

1. Service to Others: Hanuman used his strengths to serve a cause greater than himself. Consider how your unique abilities can contribute to the well-being of others. Engaging in acts of service can provide a deeper sense of purpose and fulfillment.

2. Leading by Example: Hanuman's actions inspired those around him. By realizing and utilizing your potential, you not only achieve personal growth but also inspire and empower others to explore their capabilities.

3. Continuous Learning and Growth: Hanuman's journey did not end with the leap to Lanka; he continued to serve and learn. Recognize that realizing your potential is an ongoing process. Stay committed to personal development and remain open to new experiences and lessons.

Reflection

Hanuman's story is a reminder that each of us possesses untapped strengths and abilities. The realization of our inner potential requires not just self-awareness but also the courage to face challenges, the support of those who believe in us, and a commitment to serving a purpose beyond ourselves. Like Hanuman, by believing in our worth and capabilities, we can leap across our own oceans of doubt and uncertainty, achieving what we once thought impossible.

CHAPTER ELEVEN

Overcoming Obstacles with Faith and Perseverance

The journey of Hanuman in the Ramayana, especially in overcoming seemingly insurmountable obstacles, offers deep insights into the power of faith and perseverance. These qualities not only enabled him to achieve the extraordinary but also serve as a guide for us to unlock our inner potential and navigate the challenges of life. Let's delve into how faith and perseverance are pivotal in overcoming obstacles, drawing inspiration from Hanuman's exemplary actions.

Faith: The Foundation of Strength

1. Unwavering Belief in a Higher Purpose: Hanuman's actions were grounded in his unwavering faith in Lord Rama and the righteousness of his mission. This deep belief provided him with the moral and spiritual foundation to face challenges head-on. Similarly, having faith in a higher purpose or in the intrinsic value of our pursuits can provide us with a compass during turbulent times.

2. Divine Support in Moments of Doubt: Hanuman's leap to Lanka was made possible by his faith in divine support. When faced with the vast ocean, it was his faith in Rama and the divine powers that emboldened him to take the leap. In our lives, faith in a higher power or in the support of the universe can give us the courage to take bold steps, even when the outcome is uncertain.

3. Seeing Beyond the Physical: Hanuman's ability to recognize Rama in his human form, where others saw only a mortal man, speaks to the vision that faith provides — the ability to see beyond the immediate, physical realities to the deeper truths that guide our existence. Cultivating faith allows us to perceive the potential for greatness within ourselves and others, even when it's not immediately apparent.

Perseverance: The Path Through Obstacles

1. Resilience in the Face of Challenges: The numerous challenges Hanuman faced, from the demons sent by Ravana to thwart his journey to the vast ocean itself, tested his resolve. His perseverance, driven by his mission to find Sita and serve Rama, showcases the strength that comes from resilience. Similarly, our journey through obstacles is made possible by our ability to persist, driven by our commitment to our goals.

2. Adaptability and Resourcefulness: Hanuman's journey was marked by his ability to adapt to new challenges, using his wit, strength, and divine gifts. Perseverance is not just about enduring but also about being resourceful and adaptable in the face of changing circumstances. It involves finding creative solutions and making the most of our innate abilities.

3. Learning from Setbacks: Each obstacle Hanuman encountered served as a lesson, strengthening him for the next challenge. Perseverance involves a willingness to learn from setbacks, using them as stepping stones rather than stumbling blocks. This growth mindset transforms challenges into opportunities for personal development.

Cultivating Faith and Perseverance

1. Daily Reflection and Meditation: Cultivate faith through daily reflection and meditation, focusing on your beliefs and the higher values that guide your life. This practice can strengthen your spiritual foundation, providing clarity and purpose.

2. Setting and Revisiting Goals: Keep your goals in sight, reminding yourself of the bigger picture and the reasons behind your pursuits. This perspective can renew your motivation and help you persevere through challenges.

3. Building a Support System: Surround yourself with individuals who share your values and support your goals. A strong community can bolster your faith and provide encouragement during difficult times.

4. Embracing Learning: View obstacles as opportunities to learn and grow. Adopting a mindset that values growth and learning can make perseverance a rewarding journey rather than a struggle.

By embracing the lessons of faith and perseverance illustrated by Hanuman's journey, we can navigate our own paths through life's obstacles with strength, courage, and a sense of purpose. Just as Hanuman realized his divine potential and overcame great challenges, we, too, can unlock our inner power and achieve our highest aspirations.

Wisdom and Humility

CHAPTER TWELVE

Hanuman's Intelligence and Wit

Hanuman's intelligence and wit are as legendary as his strength and devotion, playing a crucial role in the success of his endeavors throughout the Ramayana. These qualities not only showcase his capability to navigate complex situations but also offer valuable lessons on the importance of intellect and adaptability in solving problems and achieving goals.

Strategic Thinking in the Search for Sita

Hanuman's mission to find Sita in Lanka required more than just physical strength; it demanded a keen intellect and strategic thinking. Understanding the risks of direct confrontation in enemy territory, Hanuman cleverly transformed into a small form to evade detection. His methodical search for Sita, while maintaining a low profile, exemplifies the importance of strategy and discretion in tackling challenging tasks.

Diplomacy and Eloquence

Upon finding Sita, Hanuman demonstrated his eloquence and diplomatic skills. He respectfully introduced himself and explained his mission, winning her trust. His choice of words and the manner of presentation were crucial in reassuring Sita of his intentions and Rama's efforts to rescue her. This incident highlights the significance of communication skills and diplomacy in building trust and conveying sensitive information effectively.

Adaptability and Resourcefulness

Hanuman's adaptability is vividly displayed during his encounter with Surasa, the mother of serpents, who was tasked by the gods to test his resolve. When Surasa widened her mouth to devour him, Hanuman enlarged his form. Realizing that overpowering her might not be the wisest strategy, he then smartly reduced his size and darted through her ear, demonstrating quick thinking and adaptability. This episode teaches the importance of being flexible and resourceful in the face of obstacles.

Courage and Intellect in Confrontation

In Lanka, when captured by Ravana's forces, Hanuman's wit was again on display. Faced with Ravana, instead of resorting to aggression, he used the opportunity to assess the enemy's strength and deliver Rama's message. Even when sentenced to have his tail set on fire, Hanuman used this to his advantage, transforming it into an opportunity to cause havoc in Lanka. His actions underscore the power of intellect in turning adverse situations to one's advantage.

Humility and the Quest for Knowledge

Despite his vast powers and intellect, Hanuman's humility in the pursuit of knowledge is inspiring. His dedication to learning, as evidenced by his decision to study scriptures under the sun god, Surya, illustrates the importance of continuous learning and intellectual humility. This attitude towards knowledge and learning underscores the belief that wisdom and understanding are infinite resources to be pursued throughout one's life.

Lessons from Hanuman's Intellect and Wit

1. Strategic Thinking: Approach problems with a strategic mindset, considering various angles and potential solutions before acting.

2. Effective Communication: Develop your communication skills, focusing on clarity, diplomacy, and empathy, especially in delicate situations.

3. Adaptability: Be open to changing your approach based on the situation, demonstrating flexibility and creativity in problem-solving.

4. Continuous Learning: Embrace a lifelong commitment to learning, recognizing that wisdom and knowledge enhance all aspects of life.

5. Intellectual Humility: Maintain humility, acknowledging that no matter how much you know, there is always more to learn and understand.

Hanuman's intelligence and wit, integral to his

achievements, remind us of the power of the mind in overcoming challenges and achieving success. By embodying these qualities in our lives, we can navigate complex situations with grace, achieve our goals, and continue to grow intellectually and spiritually.

The Virtue of Humility in Strength

Hanuman's story is a compelling narrative that intertwines immense physical strength with the profound virtue of humility. This juxtaposition offers a powerful lesson on the essence of true strength and the importance of humility in leadership, personal growth, and spiritual development. Hanuman's humility, despite his unparalleled powers, sets a precedent for understanding the role of modesty in harnessing one's abilities for the greater good.

Humility Despite Great Power

Hanuman possessed extraordinary abilities; he could lift mountains, leap across oceans, and assume any form at will. Yet, his most defining trait was his humility. He never sought recognition for his deeds; his actions were always in service to Lord Rama and the greater purpose of restoring dharma (righteousness). This humility in the face of immense strength teaches us the importance of grounding our abilities in the service of others, rather than in the pursuit of personal glory.

The Recognition of One's Role in a Larger Purpose

Hanuman's humility was also evident in his recognition of his role within the larger cosmic play. Despite being a pivotal figure in the Ramayana, he always viewed his actions as part of Lord Rama's divine mission, never overestimating his importance. This perspective teaches the value of understanding our role in the larger scheme of things, promoting a humble approach to our contributions and achievements.

The Balance Between Confidence and Humility

Hanuman's journey also illustrates the balance between confidence in one's abilities and the virtue of humility. His leap to Lanka, for instance, was a moment of great self-assurance, driven by his devotion and the necessity of the mission. However, this confidence was always tempered with humility, never crossing into arrogance. This balance is a crucial lesson in how to approach challenges with confidence while remaining grounded in humility.

Humility as a Form of Strength

In many traditions, humility is viewed not as a weakness but as a form of strength. Hanuman embodies this principle, using his humility to forge deeper connections, inspire trust, and encourage others. His humility made him approachable and respected, highlighting how true leadership and strength are rooted in the respect and care for others.

The Impact of Humility on Personal Growth

Finally, Hanuman's humility facilitated his own spiritual growth and understanding. He was always a learner, seeking knowledge and wisdom, which is evident in his devotion to his studies and his teachers. This aspect of humility — being open to learning and acknowledging that there is always more to understand — is vital for personal and spiritual development.

Integrating Humility into Our Lives

1. Service to Others: Emulate Hanuman's example by finding joy and purpose in serving others, letting go of the need for acknowledgment or praise.

2. Self-awareness: Cultivate a keen awareness of your strengths and weaknesses, acknowledging that every individual has a unique role and contribution.

3. Balance Confidence with Modesty: Approach your tasks with confidence in your abilities, but temper that confidence with humility, acknowledging the contributions of others.

4. Continuous Learning: Maintain a posture of learning, open to new insights and willing to admit when you don't have all the answers.

5. Empathy and Compassion: Let humility guide your interactions with others, fostering empathy and compassion by placing yourself in their shoes.

Hanuman's humility, in tandem with his strength, offers

profound lessons on the essence of true power. It teaches that the greatest strength lies in selfless service, a humble approach to one's abilities, and the continuous pursuit of growth and understanding. By embodying these lessons, we can navigate life's challenges with grace and make meaningful contributions to our communities and the world at large.

Part III: Embodying Hanuman's Qualities in Personal Growth

Courage and Confidence

CHAPTER FOURTEEN

Facing Your Fears

Facing fears is a crucial step in personal growth and achieving one's potential, a lesson vividly illustrated through Hanuman's experiences. Hanuman, despite his divine powers and heroic status, encountered moments that tested his courage and resolve. His journey offers valuable insights into confronting and overcoming fears, demonstrating that courage is not the absence of fear but the determination to act in spite of it.

Acknowledging the Fear

Hanuman's initial hesitation to leap across the ocean to Lanka highlights the importance of acknowledging fear. Before making the leap, Hanuman had to confront the vastness of the ocean and the uncertainty of what lay ahead. It was through acknowledging his apprehension and understanding the necessity of his mission that he could gather the courage to act. This teaches us that recognizing and accepting our fears is the first step towards overcoming them.

Drawing Strength from Devotion and Purpose

Hanuman's devotion to Rama and his commitment to the mission of finding Sita provided him with the strength to face his fears. His leap across the ocean was fueled not just by his physical abilities but by his unwavering faith and the purpose behind his action. This illustrates how a strong sense of purpose and dedication to something greater than oneself can be powerful motivators in overcoming fears.

The Role of Support and Encouragement

The encouragement Hanuman received from Jambavan, who reminded him of his forgotten powers, played a crucial role in overcoming his hesitation. This support helped Hanuman realize his own strength and capabilities, giving him the confidence to take the leap. It underscores the importance of having a supportive community or mentor that believes in us and can help us see our own potential, especially in moments of doubt.

Transforming Fear into Action

Hanuman's transformation from hesitation to action demonstrates the power of converting fear into a driving force. By focusing on the importance of his mission and trusting in his abilities, he was able to channel his apprehension into a decisive action. This teaches us that fear, when harnessed correctly, can become a catalyst for taking bold steps towards our goals.

Learning from the Experience

After successfully leaping across the ocean and accomplishing his mission in Lanka, Hanuman's confidence and understanding of his abilities grew. This experience of facing and overcoming his fear had a transformative effect, preparing him for future challenges. It highlights how confronting our fears can lead to personal growth, self-awareness, and increased resilience.

Integrating the Lesson into Our Lives

1. Self-reflection: Spend time understanding your fears and their origins. Acknowledging and accepting your fears is the first step towards addressing them.

2. Find your purpose: Like Hanuman, let your actions be guided by a sense of purpose. Strong motivation can help you overcome apprehension.

3. Seek support: Don't hesitate to reach out for encouragement and advice from friends, family, or mentors. A supportive community can be a significant source of strength.

4. Take small steps: Facing your fears doesn't always require a leap across the ocean. Small, manageable actions towards confronting your fears can build confidence over time.

5. Reflect on your successes: After facing a fear, take time to reflect on the experience and the growth it brought. This can bolster your confidence for future challenges.

Hanuman's story teaches us that facing our fears is not only possible but essential for personal development and fulfilling our potential. By acknowledging our fears, drawing strength from our purpose, seeking support, and taking action, we can overcome obstacles and grow in confidence and resilience.

CHAPTER FIFTEEN

Building Confidence Through Action

Building confidence through action is a powerful concept embodied in Hanuman's journey, particularly evident in his leap to Lanka and his endeavors thereafter. This principle suggests that confidence is not merely a trait one possesses but is built and reinforced through deliberate, purposeful actions. Hanuman's story offers insightful lessons on how engaging in actions aligned with our values and goals can significantly enhance our self-confidence and ability to face challenges.

Starting with a Leap of Faith

Hanuman's leap to Lanka is a literal and metaphorical leap of faith, demonstrating that the first step towards building confidence is often taking action despite uncertainty. This leap required not only physical strength but immense mental fortitude and trust in his abilities. It teaches us that stepping out of our comfort zones and confronting our fears head-on can lead to significant personal growth and a boost in confidence.

Action Reinforces Self-Belief

Each action Hanuman undertook in his quest — from finding Sita to confronting demons in Lanka — reinforced his belief in his capabilities. With every challenge he faced, his confidence in his divine powers and his purpose grew stronger. This underscores the idea that confidence is cultivated through experiences and achievements, no matter how small. Engaging in actions that challenge us and push our boundaries can reinforce our self-belief and confidence.

Learning from Success and Failure

Hanuman's encounters, including both his successes and the obstacles he faced, contributed to his confidence. For instance, his ability to outwit demons and survive various challenges in Lanka showed him the extent of his capabilities. This aspect of his journey highlights the importance of learning from both successes and failures. Each experience provides valuable lessons that can build confidence, teaching us resilience and the ability to adapt and persevere.

The Role of Reflection in Building Confidence

After the successful completion of his mission, Hanuman's reflection on his journey — from his initial doubts to his ultimate success — likely contributed to his evolving self-confidence. This reflection process is crucial for internalizing the lessons learned from our actions, understanding our strengths, and recognizing areas for growth. Reflecting on our actions and their outcomes helps solidify the confidence gained from our experiences.

Cultivating Confidence in Others

Hanuman's confidence had a ripple effect, inspiring confidence in Rama, Sita, and his companions. This highlights an important aspect of building confidence through action: our actions can not only bolster our own confidence but can also inspire and uplift those around us. Demonstrating courage and resilience in the face of challenges can motivate others to believe in their abilities and take bold steps towards their goals.

Integrating These Lessons into Daily Life

1. Embrace Challenges: Seek out opportunities that push you out of your comfort zone. Each challenge you overcome builds your confidence.

2. Reflect on Your Actions: Regularly reflect on your actions, the outcomes, and the lessons learned. This reflection helps reinforce the confidence gained from your experiences.

3. Celebrate Small Wins: Recognize and celebrate your achievements, no matter how small. Acknowledging your successes reinforces self-belief.

4. Learn from Failures: View failures as opportunities for growth. Analyzing what went wrong and how you can improve builds resilience and confidence.

5. Support Others: Share your experiences and support

those around you. Building others' confidence can also reinforce your own.

Hanuman's story vividly illustrates that confidence is built through action, reinforced by successes and failures, and nurtured by reflection and support. By embodying these principles, we can cultivate a deep-seated confidence that empowers us to achieve our goals and overcome obstacles, much like Hanuman did in his timeless journey.

Devotion and Dedication

The Power of Purpose

The power of purpose is a fundamental theme in Hanuman's epic journey, particularly highlighted in his unwavering devotion to Lord Rama and his mission. This sense of purpose not only guided Hanuman's actions but also imbued him with extraordinary strength, resilience, and clarity. Drawing from Hanuman's example, we can glean valuable insights into how a strong sense of purpose can transform our capabilities and drive us to achieve remarkable feats.

Purpose as a Source of Strength

Hanuman's dedication to finding Sita and supporting Rama is a testament to how purpose can serve as a profound source of strength. When faced with the vast ocean that separated him from Lanka, it was his purpose — his commitment to Rama's cause — that empowered him to make the impossible leap. This illustrates that when our actions are fueled by a clear and meaningful purpose, we can tap into reservoirs of strength and determination we may not have known we possessed.

Clarity and Focus

A clear purpose not only provides motivation but also sharpens focus, enabling us to navigate challenges with precision and determination. Hanuman's mission was clear: to find Sita and convey Rama's message. This clarity allowed him to navigate the complexities of Lanka, devise strategies to find Sita, and ultimately succeed in his mission. Similarly, a well-defined purpose can help us maintain focus on our goals, guiding our actions and decisions towards achieving them.

Resilience in the Face of Adversity

Hanuman encountered numerous obstacles, from demons and dangerous creatures to the burning of his tail in Lanka. It was his unwavering purpose that fostered resilience, enabling him to persevere through these challenges. Purpose instills a sense of commitment that can sustain us through difficulties, reminding us of the 'why' behind our endeavors and giving us the fortitude to continue, even when the path is fraught with obstacles.

Inspiration and Influence

Hanuman's purpose-driven actions not only contributed to the success of his mission but also served as an inspiration to others. His dedication and achievements inspired confidence and courage in Rama's army, rallying them towards their collective goal. When we lead with purpose, we not only elevate our own potential but also inspire those around us to pursue their goals with renewed vigor and determination.

Nurturing a Sense of Purpose

1. Self-reflection: Regularly engage in self-reflection to understand what truly matters to you. Identifying your values and passions can help clarify your purpose.

2. Set Meaningful Goals: Align your goals with your purpose, ensuring that they reflect what you stand for and aspire to achieve. This alignment can provide a sense of direction and fulfillment.

3. Embrace Challenges: View challenges as opportunities to fulfill your purpose. Each obstacle overcome brings you closer to your goal, reinforcing your commitment.

4. Seek Inspiration: Look to stories of individuals like Hanuman or others who have pursued their purposes with dedication. Their journeys can offer valuable lessons and inspiration.

5. Contribute to Others: Extend your purpose beyond personal achievement to include the well-being and upliftment of others. Serving a cause greater than oneself can deepen your sense of purpose and fulfillment.

Hanuman's journey underscores the transformative power of purpose. A strong sense of purpose not only fuels our inner strength and resilience but also brings clarity and focus to our endeavors. By cultivating a purpose-driven life, we can navigate the complexities of our journey with determination, inspire those around us, and achieve a sense of fulfillment and accomplishment that transcends ordinary achievements.

CHAPTER SEVENTEEN

Living a Life of Service and Devotion

Living a life of service and devotion, exemplified by Hanuman's dedication to Lord Rama, provides a profound framework for achieving fulfillment and spiritual growth. Hanuman's actions, motivated by selfless service and unwavering devotion, highlight the transformative impact of dedicating one's life to serving others and a higher purpose. This path not only enriches the lives of others but also cultivates inner peace, happiness, and a deep sense of purpose in one's own life.

Embracing Service as a Path to Fulfillment

1. Selflessness: Hanuman's service to Rama was marked by selflessness. He sought no recognition or reward, focusing solely on the well-being and success of Rama. Adopting a selfless approach to service can lead to profound personal satisfaction, as the act of giving becomes its own reward.

2. Empathy and Compassion: At the heart of Hanuman's service was his deep empathy and compassion for Rama and Sita's plight. By nurturing empathy, we can better understand and address the needs of those we serve, fostering a more compassionate world.

3. Dedication and Perseverance: Hanuman's journey was fraught with challenges, yet his dedication never wavered. This teaches us the value of perseverance in service, committing wholeheartedly to our cause or mission, even in the face of obstacles.

Cultivating Devotion in Everyday Life

1. Daily Practices: Incorporate practices that nurture devotion, such as meditation, prayer, or chanting, into your daily routine. These practices can help you connect with a higher purpose and cultivate a sense of devotion in all aspects of life.

2. Mindful Actions: Approach your daily activities with mindfulness and intention, seeing them as opportunities to serve and express devotion. Whether it's helping a colleague, volunteering in your community, or supporting a loved one, each action can be imbued with the spirit of service.

3. Gratitude: Cultivate gratitude for the opportunity to serve and for the guidance of the higher powers or principles you are devoted to. Gratitude can deepen your connection to your purpose and the joy derived from service.

The Impact of Service and Devotion

1. Personal Growth: Engaging in service and devotion

promotes personal growth, encouraging qualities like humility, patience, and resilience. These qualities not only enhance our capacity for service but also our overall well-being and happiness.

2. Community and Connection: Living a life of service and devotion fosters a sense of community and connection, both with those we serve and with fellow practitioners. This sense of belonging can be a powerful source of support and inspiration.

3. Spiritual Development: Service and devotion are pathways to spiritual development, offering insights into the nature of the self, the interconnectedness of all beings, and the presence of the divine in everyday life. This spiritual awareness can bring peace and fulfillment.

Integrating Service and Devotion into Your Life

Identify Your Passions: Align your service with your passions and interests. Serving in areas that resonate with you can be more fulfilling and impactful.

Set Realistic Goals: Start with small, achievable goals for your service and devotion practices. Gradual integration can lead to lasting habits and deeper commitment.

Seek Community: Engage with communities or groups that share your commitment to service and devotion. These connections can provide encouragement, ideas, and support.

Living a life of service and devotion, as Hanuman

exemplifies, offers a path to personal and spiritual fulfillment. By serving others and dedicating ourselves to a higher purpose, we can discover deeper meaning in our lives, cultivate lasting happiness, and contribute to the well-being of the world around us.

Strength and Resilience

Cultivating Physical and Mental Strength

Cultivating physical and mental strength is essential for navigating the challenges of life with resilience, agility, and a clear mind. Hanuman, embodying the pinnacle of both physical prowess and mental acuity, provides a profound example of how these strengths can be developed and harmonized. Inspired by Hanuman's journey, let's explore practical ways to cultivate physical and mental strength in our own lives.

Physical Strength: Building a Foundation

1. Regular Exercise: Incorporate a balanced regimen of cardiovascular, strength, flexibility, and balance training into your routine. Exercises like running, swimming, yoga, and weight training can enhance physical endurance, strength, and flexibility, mirroring Hanuman's agility and might.

2. Nutrition: Prioritize a nutritious diet that fuels your body and supports your physical activities. Emulate the vitality provided by the sun to Hanuman by consuming a variety of fruits, vegetables, whole grains, lean proteins, and healthy fats, ensuring your body receives the essential nutrients it needs to thrive.

3. Rest and Recovery: Just as Hanuman had moments of rest, understand the importance of rest and recovery in enhancing physical performance and preventing injuries. Ensure adequate sleep, engage in restorative practices like yoga or meditation, and listen to your body's needs for downtime.

Mental Strength: Sharpening the Mind

1. Meditation and Mindfulness: Engage in daily meditation and mindfulness practices to develop mental clarity, concentration, and peace, akin to Hanuman's focused and serene mind. These practices can help manage stress, enhance cognitive functions, and foster emotional resilience.

2. Continuous Learning: Cultivate a mindset of continuous learning and curiosity. Engage with new ideas, skills, and knowledge areas to keep your mind sharp and adaptable. Hanuman's quest for knowledge under the sun god Surya exemplifies the importance of lifelong learning.

3. Resilience Training: Develop resilience by challenging yourself to step out of your comfort zone, whether through physical challenges, new hobbies, or setting and pursuing ambitious goals. Overcoming these challenges can strengthen your mental fortitude and confidence.

4. Positive Relationships: Foster supportive and positive relationships that encourage personal growth and provide emotional support during challenging times. The bond between Hanuman, Rama, and their allies highlights the strength found in camaraderie and shared purpose.

5. Service and Devotion: Like Hanuman's devotion to Rama and his cause, find a cause or purpose beyond yourself that you can serve. Engaging in volunteer work or contributing to your community can provide a sense of purpose and fulfillment, strengthening your resolve and sense of belonging.

Integrating Physical and Mental Strength

Integrated Practices: Engage in activities that combine physical and mental disciplines, such as martial arts, yoga, or dance. These practices can help harmonize the body and mind, fostering a holistic sense of strength and well-being.

Routine and Discipline: Establish a disciplined routine for your physical and mental practices, ensuring consistency and progress. Discipline was key to Hanuman's strength and accomplishments.

Reflection and Adjustment: Regularly reflect on your progress and be open to adjusting your practices as needed. This reflective process ensures that your approach to building strength remains aligned with your goals and needs.

By embodying the lessons from Hanuman's life, we can cultivate a balanced approach to strengthening our bodies and minds. This holistic strength not only prepares us to face life's challenges but also enables us to pursue our goals with vigor, resilience, and clarity.

CHAPTER NINETEEN

The Art of Resilience in Adversity

The art of resilience in adversity, as exemplified by Hanuman's journey, offers profound insights into facing life's challenges with courage, adaptability, and unwavering determination. Hanuman's ability to overcome obstacles, whether it's finding Sita, crossing the ocean, or fighting in the battle against Ravana, demonstrates the essence of resilience. Drawing from his example, we can cultivate resilience in our own lives, turning adversity into a catalyst for growth and transformation.

Understanding Resilience

Resilience is the capacity to recover quickly from difficulties, adapting in the face of adversity, trauma, tragedy, or significant sources of stress. It involves a combination of mental toughness, emotional strength, and a deep-rooted sense of purpose. Like Hanuman, resilient individuals view challenges as opportunities to demonstrate their strength and adaptability.

Cultivating Resilience

1. Develop a Strong Sense of Purpose: Hanuman's actions were driven by his devotion to Lord Rama and his mission. A strong sense of purpose can provide clarity and motivation during challenging times, acting as a guiding light that keeps you focused and determined.

2. Embrace Flexibility: Hanuman's ability to change his form and approach as needed highlights the importance of adaptability. Embrace flexibility in your strategies and thinking, allowing you to navigate through challenges more effectively.

3. Foster Optimism: Maintaining a positive outlook, even in the face of adversity, can significantly impact your resilience. Optimism doesn't mean ignoring reality but rather maintaining hope and focusing on solutions rather than dwelling on problems.

4. Build Emotional Intelligence: Hanuman's interactions show his empathy, understanding, and control over his emotions. Cultivating emotional intelligence helps in managing stress, empathizing with others, and maintaining emotional balance.

5. Seek Support and Offer It to Others: Just as Hanuman relied on his allies and offered them unwavering support, building strong relationships can provide emotional support and encouragement. Don't hesitate to seek help when needed, and be there for others, fostering a supportive network.

6. Learn from Experiences: Every challenge Hanuman

faced taught him something valuable. View obstacles as learning opportunities, reflecting on what they teach you about yourself, your capabilities, and how you can grow from the experience.

7. Practice Self-Care: Taking care of your physical, emotional, and spiritual well-being is crucial for resilience. Regular exercise, meditation, healthy eating, and engaging in activities that bring you joy can strengthen your ability to withstand stress.

8. Set Realistic Goals and Take Action: Hanuman's journey was marked by clear objectives and decisive actions. Set achievable goals and work towards them systematically, taking small, manageable steps. This approach can help build momentum and a sense of accomplishment.

Living with Resilience

Incorporating resilience into your life is a dynamic process that requires mindfulness, patience, and practice. It's about building a toolkit of strategies that you can draw upon, much like Hanuman's varied powers and abilities, to adapt and thrive in the face of life's uncertainties. Remember, resilience is not just about bouncing back; it's about growing, learning, and emerging stronger from the challenges you face.

By embodying the principles of resilience demonstrated by Hanuman, we can approach life's adversities not as insurmountable obstacles but as opportunities for personal growth, development, and transformation.

Part IV: Practical Applications

Meditation and Mantras

CHAPTER TWENTY

Connecting with Hanuman Through Meditation

Connecting with Hanuman through meditation can be a deeply spiritual practice that offers inspiration, strength, and inner peace. Hanuman embodies qualities such as devotion, courage, strength, and humility, making him an ideal focus for meditation for those seeking to cultivate these virtues within themselves. Here's a guide to help you connect with Hanuman through meditation, drawing upon the essence of his character and teachings.

Preparing for Meditation

1. Find a Quiet Space: Choose a quiet and comfortable place where you won't be disturbed. This space should feel safe and sacred to you.

2. Set the Ambiance: Consider lighting a candle or incense to create a serene atmosphere. You might also want to have an image or statue of Hanuman in your meditation space as a focal point.

3. Sit Comfortably: Sit in a comfortable position, with your spine straight but not tense. You can sit on the floor with a cushion or on a chair with your feet flat on the ground.

Focusing Your Intentions

1. Set Your Intention: Begin by setting an intention for your meditation. This could be to cultivate a specific quality of Hanuman, such as strength, devotion, or humility, or simply to connect with his energy and guidance.

2. Breathing Deeply: Close your eyes and take several deep breaths to center yourself. With each breath, feel yourself becoming more relaxed and open.

Visualization Meditation

1. Visualizing Hanuman: In your mind's eye, visualize Hanuman in front of you. Imagine him with his mighty form, full of strength and compassion. See his gentle smile and the warmth in his eyes that reflect his deep devotion.

2. Connecting with Qualities: Focus on the qualities of Hanuman that resonate with you. It could be his unwavering devotion to Lord Rama, his immense strength, his courage to face challenges, or his profound humility.

3. Absorbing Virtues: Imagine the qualities of Hanuman as a radiant light emanating from him. With each breath, visualize this light entering your heart, filling you with the same virtues. Feel these qualities becoming a part of you, strengthening and inspiring you.

Chanting Meditation

1. Chanting the Hanuman Chalisa or Mantras: If you're familiar with the Hanuman Chalisa, you can chant it as a form of meditation. Alternatively, you can chant simple mantras dedicated to Hanuman, such as "Om Hanumate Namah" or "Jai Hanuman."

2. Absorbing the Vibrations: As you chant, focus on the sound and vibration of the words, allowing them to fill you with energy and peace. Feel the presence of Hanuman growing stronger around you, enveloping you in his blessings.

Reflective Meditation

1. Reflect on Hanuman's Stories: Think about the stories of Hanuman's adventures and the lessons they hold. Reflect on how these stories apply to your life and the challenges you face.

2. Seeking Guidance: Silently ask Hanuman for guidance or support in areas of your life where you need strength, courage, or devotion. Open your heart to any insights or feelings that arise.

Closing the Meditation

1. Expressing Gratitude: Conclude your meditation by expressing gratitude to Hanuman for his presence and the qualities he has shared with you. Feel gratitude for the opportunity to connect with these virtues within yourself.

2. Returning Gently: Take a few deep breaths and slowly bring your awareness back to the present moment. When you feel ready, gently open your eyes, carrying the strength and peace from the meditation into your day.

Connecting with Hanuman through meditation is a powerful way to draw upon his divine virtues, offering us strength, guidance, and inspiration on our spiritual journey. By regularly engaging in this practice, we can deepen our connection to Hanuman and embody the qualities that he represents in our own lives.

The Hanuman Chalisa: A Spiritual Tool for Empowerment

The Hanuman Chalisa, composed by the 16th-century poet-saint Tulsidas, is a powerful devotional hymn dedicated to Lord Hanuman. It consists of 40 verses (Chalisa comes from "chalis," meaning forty in Hindi) that detail Hanuman's unparalleled devotion to Lord Rama, his incredible feats, and his gracious strength. This hymn is not just a tribute to Hanuman's glory but serves as a spiritual tool for empowerment, offering solace, strength, and inspiration to devotees across generations.

Doha

Shri Guru Charan Sarooja-raj Nija manu Mukura Sudhaari
Baranau Rahubhara Bimala Yasha Jo Dayaka Phala Chari
Budhee-Heen Thanu Jannikay Sumirow Pavana Kumara
Bala-Budhee Vidya Dehoo Mohee Harahu Kalesha Vikaara

Chopai

Jai Hanuman gyan gun saga	Jai Kapis tihun lok ujagar
Ram doot atulit bal dhama	Anjaani-putra Pavan sut nama
Mahabir Bikram Bajrang	Kumati nivar sumati Ke sangi
Kanchan varan viraj subesa	Kanan Kundal Kunchit Kesha
Hath Vajra Aur Dhuvaje Viraje	Kaandhe moonj janehu sajai
Sankar suvan kesri Nandan	Tej prataap maha jag vandan
Vidyavaan guni ati chatur	Ram kaj karibe ko aatur
Prabu charitra sunibe-ko rasiya	Ram Lakhan Sita man Basiya
Sukshma roop dhari Siyahi dikhava	Vikat roop dhari lank jarava
Bhima roop dhari asur sanghare	Ramachandra ke kaj sanvare
Laye Sanjivan Lakhan Jiyaye	Shri Raghuvir Harashi ur laye
Raghupati Kinhi bahut badai	Tum mam priye Bharat-hi-sam bhai
Sahas badan tumharo yash gave	Asa-kahi Shripati kanth lagaave
Sankadhik Brahmaadi Muneesa	Narad-Sarad sahit Aheesa
Yam Kuber Digpaal Jahan te	Kavi kovid kahi sake kahan te
Tum upkar Sugreevahin keenha	Ram milaye rajpad deenha
Tumharo mantra Vibheeshan maana	Lankeshwar Bhaye Sub jag jana
Yug sahastra jojan par Bhanu	Leelyo tahi madhur phal janu
Prabhu mudrika meli mukh mahee	Jaladhi langhi gaye achraj nahee
Durgaam kaj jagath ke jete	Sugam anugraha tumhre tete
Ram dwaare tum rakhvare	Hoat na agya binu paisare
Sub sukh lahae tumhari sar na	Tum rakshak kahu ko dar naa
Aapan tej samharo aapai	Teenhon lok hank te kanpai
Bhoot pisaach Nikat nahin aavai	Mahavir jab naam sunavae
Nase rog harae sab peera	Japat nirantar Hanumant beera
Sankat se Hanuman chudavae	Man Karam Vachan dyan jo lavai
Sab par Ram tapasvee raja	Tin ke kaj sakal Tum saja
Aur manorath jo koi lavai	Sohi amit jeevan phal pavai
Charon Yug partap tumhara	Hai persidh jagat ujiyara
Sadhu Sant ke tum Rakhware	Asur nikandan Ram dulhare
Ashta-sidhi nav nidhi ke dhata	As-var deen Janki mata
Ram rasayan tumhare pasa	Sada raho Raghupati ke dasa
Tumhare bhajan Ram ko pavai	Janam-janam ke dukh bisraavai
Anth-kaal Raghuvir pur jayee	Jahan janam Hari-Bakht Kahayee
Aur Devta Chit na dharehi	Hanumanth se hi sarve sukh karehi
Sankat kate-mite sab peera	Jo sumirai Hanumat Balbeera
Jai Jai Jai Hanuman Gosahin	Kripa Karahu Gurudev ki nyahin
Jo sat bar path kare kohi	Chutehi bandhi maha sukh hohi
Jo yah padhe Hanuman Chalisa	Hoye siddhi sakhi Gaureesa
Tulsidas sada hari chera	Keejai Nath Hridaye mein dera

Doha

Pavantnaye sankat haran, Mangal murti roop |
Ram lakhan sita sahet, Hridaye basau sur bhup ||

Let's explore how the Hanuman Chalisa can be a source of empowerment and the ways in which it can enhance one's spiritual practice.

Spiritual Empowerment through the Hanuman Chalisa

1. Cultivating Courage and Strength: Reciting the Hanuman Chalisa is believed to infuse the devotee with Hanuman's courage and strength. The verses narrate his fearless endeavors, serving as a reminder of the power of devotion and the strength that comes from faith and righteousness. This can be particularly empowering in times of fear, anxiety, or when facing life's challenges.

2. Protection from Negative Energies: Many believe that chanting the Hanuman Chalisa offers protection against negative influences and spirits. Hanuman's role as a guardian and protector is celebrated in several verses, providing a sense of security to those who recite the hymn with devotion.

3. Removal of Obstacles: The hymn praises Hanuman's ability to remove obstacles and bring success in endeavors. By chanting the Chalisa, devotees seek Hanuman's blessings in overcoming difficulties and hurdles in their path, both spiritual and material.

4. Fostering Devotion and Spiritual Growth: The Hanuman Chalisa is a testament to the power of Bhakti (devotion). It encourages the cultivation of devotion not just towards Hanuman or Rama but as a fundamental spiritual practice. This deepening of devotion can lead to profound inner transformation and alignment with one's higher self.

5. Healing and Well-being: The act of chanting or listening to the Chalisa can have a soothing effect on the mind and body. The rhythmic verses and the meditative practice of chanting can aid in reducing stress, promoting mental clarity, and enhancing overall well-being.

Incorporating the Hanuman Chalisa into Your Spiritual Practice

1. Daily Recitation: Establishing a daily practice of reciting the Hanuman Chalisa, especially in the morning or at dusk, can help start or end your day with a sense of peace and purpose.

2. Meditative Chanting: Use the Chalisa as a form of meditation. Focus on the meaning of each verse as you chant, allowing the qualities of Hanuman to permeate your consciousness.

3. Listening with Intent: If you are not familiar with the verses, listening to recordings of the Chalisa can also be beneficial. Listen attentively, focusing on the words and their meanings, and allowing the vibrations to uplift your spirit.

4. Understanding the Verses: Taking time to study the meanings of the verses can deepen your connection to the hymn. This understanding can transform your recitation into a more profound, introspective practice.

5. Group Recitation: Chanting the Hanuman Chalisa in a

group can amplify its effects, creating a collective energy that enhances the sense of community and shared devotion.

The Hanuman Chalisa is more than just a set of verses in praise of Lord Hanuman; it is a spiritual tool that empowers individuals to face life's adversities with courage, clarity, and a profound sense of devotion. Whether through chanting, listening, or meditative reflection, engaging with the Chalisa can bring about spiritual upliftment, protection, and a deeper connection to the divine. It stands as a beacon of hope, strength, and resilience, guiding devotees on their spiritual journey.

Lessons from the Epic Ramayana

CHAPTER TWENTY-TWO

Applying Hanuman's Lessons in Modern Life

Incorporating the lessons from Hanuman's life into modern existence can provide valuable insights for navigating contemporary challenges with grace, strength, and integrity. Hanuman embodies virtues such as unwavering devotion, immense courage, selfless service, and intellectual prowess, all of which are as relevant today as they were in the ancient epic. Here's how we can apply Hanuman's teachings to our lives in today's world.

Cultivating Unwavering Devotion

Hanuman's devotion to Lord Rama is legendary, serving as a powerful example of loyalty and faithfulness. In a modern context, this can translate to dedication in our relationships, careers, and personal goals. It teaches us the importance of commitment, urging us to approach our responsibilities with a sense of purpose and devotion.

Practical Application: Cultivate dedication in your personal and professional life by setting clear intentions, staying true to your values, and being present and engaged in your interactions and tasks.

Embracing Courage and Strength

Hanuman's courage in the face of daunting challenges is inspirational. Today, we face our own set of challenges, from personal struggles to global issues. Hanuman's story encourages us to face these with courage, utilizing our inner strength to overcome obstacles.

Practical Application: When faced with difficult situations, remind yourself of your inner strength. Approach challenges with a positive mindset, and don't hesitate to seek support when needed, just as Hanuman did.

Practicing Selfless Service

The essence of Hanuman's actions lies in selflessness. His life was a testament to serving others without expecting anything in return. In an increasingly self-centered world, Hanuman's example prompts us to look beyond our desires and work towards the greater good.

Practical Application: Volunteer for causes you care about, help those in need without expecting recognition, and make decisions that benefit not just yourself but also the community and environment.

Exercising Intellectual Wisdom

Hanuman was not only physically strong but also intellectually gifted. His wisdom and ability to think critically were crucial in his search for Sita and in overcoming obstacles. This highlights the importance of nurturing our minds and using our intelligence to solve problems.

Practical Application: Invest in lifelong learning, practice critical thinking, and approach problems with creativity and open-mindedness. Engage in discussions and read widely to enhance your understanding of the world.

Maintaining Humility

Despite his immense powers, Hanuman remained humble, a trait that endeared him to all. This humility in the face of greatness is a powerful lesson in an age where ego often takes precedence.

Practical Application: Practice humility by acknowledging the contributions of others, being open to learning from different sources, and recognizing that everyone has something valuable to offer.

Fostering Resilience and Adaptability

Hanuman's journey was filled with unforeseen challenges, yet his resilience and adaptability allowed him to navigate these successfully. As we encounter rapid changes and uncertainties in our own lives, Hanuman's adaptability serves as a guiding principle.

Practical Application: Cultivate resilience by staying flexible, embracing change, and viewing failures as opportunities for growth. Develop coping strategies that allow you to bounce back from setbacks.

By integrating these timeless lessons from Hanuman's life into our daily practices, we can navigate the complexities of modern life with a balanced approach, embodying strength, wisdom, and compassion. Hanuman's example offers a blueprint for living that is not only fulfilling but also enriches those around us, fostering a life of purpose, service, and devotion.

CHAPTER TWENTY-THREE

Overcoming Personal Challenges with Grace and Strength

Hanuman's journey, marked by formidable challenges overcome with grace and strength, offers timeless lessons applicable to modern life. His story is not just about physical might but also about inner strength, resilience, and the power of devotion. By drawing upon Hanuman's virtues and experiences, we can navigate personal challenges more effectively, embodying his grace and strength in our lives.

Embracing Courage and Resilience

Hanuman's leap to Lanka, despite the daunting expanse of the ocean, teaches us the value of courage in the face of uncertainty. Modern life, with its rapid changes and unpredictable challenges, requires a similar leap of faith at times. Whether it's changing careers, moving to a new place, or facing personal trials, embracing courage and resilience, as Hanuman did, can propel us forward. The key is to recognize our inner strength and take that leap, trusting in our abilities and the support system around us.

Cultivating Devotion and Purpose

At the heart of Hanuman's actions was his unwavering devotion to Lord Rama and his purpose. This devotion gave him clarity and strength, guiding him through challenges. In modern life, identifying what we are truly devoted to — be it personal goals, relationships, or causes — can provide a sense of purpose that motivates and sustains us. When we align our actions with our deeper values and purpose, we find the strength to overcome obstacles and the grace to navigate life's complexities.

Leveraging Adaptability and Intelligence

Hanuman's journey was also a testament to his adaptability and intelligence, from navigating his way through Lanka to devising strategies to confront obstacles. Similarly, in today's fast-paced world, adaptability and critical thinking are crucial. Facing personal challenges with grace involves being open to new solutions, thinking creatively, and being willing to adjust our strategies as circumstances evolve.

Practicing Humility and Selflessness

Despite his immense power, Hanuman always acted with humility and a focus on service. This teaches us the importance of humility in our own successes and strengths. True strength lies in using our abilities for the greater good, supporting others, and recognizing that we are part of a larger community. In facing personal challenges, adopting a mindset of service and humility can lead to more meaningful and fulfilling outcomes.

Finding Strength in Faith and Spirituality

For Hanuman, faith was a source of unparalleled strength. In our lives, too, spirituality or faith can be a powerful force in overcoming challenges. Whether it's through meditation, prayer, or reflection, connecting with a higher power or our inner spirituality can provide comfort, guidance, and resilience in difficult times.

Implementing Hanuman's Lessons

1. Face challenges with courage, recognizing that each obstacle is an opportunity for growth.

2. Clarify your purpose, and let it guide your decisions and actions.

3. Stay adaptable, open to learning and adjusting your approach as needed.

4. Act with humility and selflessness, focusing on how your actions can benefit others.

5. Draw strength from your faith or spirituality, finding comfort and guidance in your beliefs.

By embodying these lessons from Hanuman's life, we can approach personal challenges with a blend of grace and strength, navigating the complexities of modern life with resilience, purpose, and a deep sense of inner peace.

Community and Belief

The Importance of Community in Spiritual Growth

The significance of community in spiritual growth is a theme that resonates deeply within the story of Hanuman and his integral role in the Ramayana. This epic not only highlights individual virtues and achievements but also underscores the profound impact of collective effort, support, and unity in overcoming challenges and accomplishing divine missions. The relationship between Hanuman, Lord Rama, and the diverse assembly of beings rallying for a common cause exemplifies how community plays a crucial role in spiritual development and achievement.

Collective Strength and Support

The endeavor to rescue Sita from Ravana required the collective efforts of Rama, Hanuman, and the vanara (monkey) army, among others. This alliance demonstrates that while individual efforts are essential, the strength of a community can amplify these efforts, making the impossible possible. Hanuman's feats, though remarkable on their own, gain greater significance within the context of his service to Rama and the support he receives from and provides to the community. This teaches us the value of seeking and offering support within our spiritual communities, emphasizing that growth often happens through shared struggles and victories.

Diversity and Unity

The community that comes together in the Ramayana is notably diverse, comprising beings from different backgrounds, species, and realms, united in their devotion to Rama and the cause of righteousness. This unity in diversity highlights the importance of inclusivity in spiritual communities. It reminds us that spiritual growth transcends superficial differences, fostering a sense of oneness and shared purpose that is essential for overcoming challenges and achieving collective goals.

Learning and Inspiration

In a spiritual community, individuals have unique strengths, experiences, and insights that can serve as sources of learning and inspiration for others. Hanuman's devotion, courage, and humility inspire others in Rama's alliance, just as their faith and efforts inspire him. This mutual inspiration is pivotal in spiritual growth, as it encourages individuals to strive for higher virtues and deepen their spiritual practices.

The Role of Satsang

In Hinduism, the concept of Satsang—being in the company of the truth or the good—emphasizes the importance of gathering with those who share spiritual aspirations. Through Satsang, or similar gatherings in other spiritual traditions, individuals can engage in discussions, practices, and rituals that reinforce their faith, offer new perspectives, and strengthen their resolve on the spiritual path. Hanuman's interactions with Rama, Sita, and his allies can be seen as a form of Satsang, where the exchange of ideas, emotions, and spiritual energy fuels their collective spiritual journey.

Fostering a Supportive Spiritual Community

1. Engage in Shared Practices: Participate in group meditations, chanting sessions, or study groups to deepen your spiritual practice with the support of a community.

2. Offer and Seek Support: Be open to offering support to those in your community and seeking help when you need it. Spiritual journeys are enriched by the compassion and assistance we extend to each other.

3. Celebrate Diversity: Embrace the diversity within your spiritual community, recognizing that each individual brings unique insights and strengths that can enrich the collective experience.

4. Cultivate Mutual Respect and Understanding: Foster an environment of respect and understanding, where members can share their experiences and beliefs openly, without fear of judgment.

5. Inspire and Be Inspired: Share your journey, the challenges you've overcome, and the lessons you've learned, allowing your story to inspire others while being open to the inspiration they provide.

The importance of community in spiritual growth, exemplified by Hanuman and the collective efforts in the Ramayana, highlights that while individual practice is vital, the support, diversity, and unity of a community can profoundly enhance our spiritual journey. In coming together, sharing our paths, and supporting each other, we can navigate the challenges of life with greater strength, grace, and wisdom.

CHAPTER TWENTY-FIVE

Fostering Belief and Faith in Oneself

Fostering belief and faith in oneself is pivotal for navigating life's challenges and achieving personal growth. Drawing inspiration from Hanuman's unwavering belief in his abilities and his deep faith in Lord Rama, we can apply these principles to cultivate a strong sense of self-belief and faith. Here's how we can integrate these lessons into our lives, fostering resilience, confidence, and a profound sense of purpose.

Recognizing Your Inner Strength

Hanuman, despite his divine powers, needed reminding of his immense capabilities before he could make the leap to Lanka. Similarly, we often underestimate our abilities and need to remind ourselves of the strength that lies within. Regular reflection on past successes and challenges overcome can reinforce our belief in our capabilities. Acknowledging your strengths and achievements, no matter how small, builds a foundation of self-belief that can empower you to tackle future obstacles.

Embracing a Higher Purpose

Just as Hanuman's actions were driven by his devotion to Rama and the pursuit of a higher purpose, finding and committing to something greater than oneself can instill a deep sense of faith and direction in life. This could be a personal mission, a passion project, or service to others. A higher purpose acts as a guiding light, providing context for your struggles and a reason to persevere, reinforcing faith in your path.

The Power of Positive Affirmations

Hanuman's confidence was bolstered by Jambavan's reminder of his divine powers. Similarly, positive affirmations can serve as daily reminders of our worth and potential. Crafting personal affirmations that resonate with your goals and aspirations, and reciting them regularly, can help shift your mindset from self-doubt to self-assurance, cultivating a belief in your ability to overcome challenges and achieve your goals.

Learning from Setbacks

Hanuman's journey was not without its challenges, yet he never saw setbacks as failures, but as opportunities to grow and adapt. Viewing your own setbacks through a similar lens can foster resilience and a deeper belief in your ability to navigate difficulties. Analyze setbacks to understand what they teach you, and apply these lessons moving forward, reinforcing your faith in your ability to learn and evolve.

Seeking and Offering Support

The support Hanuman received from his allies was crucial in his endeavors. Likewise, surrounding yourself with a supportive community can bolster your belief and faith in yourself. Seek out mentors, peers, and friends who encourage and believe in you, and offer the same support to others. Sharing experiences and learning from others' journeys can strengthen your faith in your own path and in the collective strength of community.

Cultivating Spiritual Practices

Hanuman's devotion to Rama was central to his strength and success. Engaging in spiritual or mindfulness practices that resonate with you can deepen your inner faith and provide strength during challenging times. Whether it's meditation, prayer, yoga, or reading spiritual texts, these practices can offer comfort, clarity, and a renewed sense of belief in your journey.

Committing to Continuous Growth

Hanuman's quest for knowledge and self-improvement is a reminder of the importance of lifelong learning in building self-belief. Embrace opportunities for growth, be open to new experiences, and continuously seek knowledge. This commitment to personal development can reinforce your faith in your capacity to evolve and adapt, no matter what challenges you face.

Fostering belief and faith in oneself is a journey of continuous reflection, learning, and growth. Inspired by

Hanuman's example, we can cultivate these qualities within ourselves, enabling us to navigate life with grace, strength, and a deep-rooted sense of purpose.

Part V: Epilogue

CHAPTER TWENTY-SIX

Reflecting on the Journey

Reflecting on our journey through the exploration of Hanuman's teachings and how they can be applied in modern life offers a profound insight into the timeless nature of these lessons. Hanuman's story, rich with devotion, strength, humility, and wisdom, serves not only as a spiritual guide but also as a practical framework for personal development and overcoming challenges.

The Essence of Devotion and Purpose

At the heart of Hanuman's narrative is his unwavering devotion to Lord Rama and his purpose. This teaches us the power of aligning with a cause greater than ourselves, driving us to transcend our limitations and act with courage and determination. The lesson for us is clear: finding and dedicating ourselves to our purpose can imbue our lives with meaning and propel us towards our goals, even in the face of adversity.

Cultivating Strength and Resilience

Hanuman's physical and mental strength, coupled with his resilience, allowed him to face daunting challenges without faltering. His journey underscores the importance of nurturing our bodies and minds, preparing us to tackle life's obstacles with grace. Regular physical activity, mindful practices, and embracing challenges as opportunities for growth are ways we can build our resilience, inspired by Hanuman's example.

The Virtue of Humility

Despite his immense power, Hanuman's humility is a lesson in the importance of grounding our achievements and abilities in service to others. His story reminds us that true greatness lies not in accolades or recognition but in our contributions to the wellbeing of others and the humility with which we carry ourselves through the world.

The Role of Community and Support

Hanuman's achievements were not solitary; they were deeply connected to his community and the support he received and offered. This highlights the significance of building and nurturing supportive relationships and communities. Whether seeking guidance, offering support, or working towards a common goal, the strength of our connections can be a powerful force in our lives.

Fostering Belief and Faith

Finally, Hanuman's unwavering belief in himself and his faith in a higher purpose offer profound lessons in self-confidence and spiritual faith. By believing in our capabilities and cultivating a deeper connection to our spiritual or personal guiding principles, we can navigate life's ups and downs with a steady heart and a clear mind.

Moving Forward

Reflecting on our journey with Hanuman teaches us that the principles of devotion, strength, humility, community, and faith are not just ideals but practical virtues that can guide our actions and decisions. As we move forward, let us carry these lessons with us, applying them to our challenges, aspirations, and interactions. In doing so, we honor the legacy of Hanuman and the timeless wisdom of his story, allowing it to illuminate our paths and inspire our spirits.

In embracing these teachings, we not only enhance our personal growth and resilience but also contribute to a more compassionate, understanding, and connected world. Hanuman's journey, therefore, becomes more than a mythological narrative; it becomes a living guide, offering us direction, strength, and hope as we navigate the complexities of modern life.

CHAPTER TWENTY-SEVEN

Hanuman: A Beacon of Hope and Strength

Hanuman stands as a timeless beacon of hope and strength, transcending cultural and spiritual boundaries to inspire countless individuals across the world. His story, rich with feats of devotion, courage, wisdom, and humility, serves not only as a spiritual guide but also as a source of practical life lessons. Hanuman's enduring legacy teaches us how to navigate life's challenges with grace, embodying the virtues that lead to personal and collective upliftment.

The Embodiment of Devotion and Selflessness

At the core of Hanuman's narrative is his unwavering devotion to Lord Rama, a devotion that fueled his every action and decision. This selflessness, devoid of any personal gain, highlights the profound impact of living a life centered on service and dedication to a cause greater than oneself. Hanuman's devotion teaches us the power of pure intention and the fulfillment that comes from serving others with a whole heart.

A Symbol of Strength and Resilience

Hanuman's physical prowess is matched only by his mental fortitude, making him an emblem of strength in all its forms. His ability to overcome insurmountable odds, whether in leaping across oceans or confronting formidable adversaries, underscores the importance of resilience. Hanuman's story encourages us to cultivate our inner strength, reminding us that we are capable of facing life's adversities with courage and determination.

Wisdom and Humility: The Marks of True Greatness

Despite his divine powers and achievements, Hanuman's humility remains one of his most revered attributes. His wisdom, born of experience and understanding, was always used in service to others, never for personal acclaim. In an age where ego often overshadows empathy, Hanuman's humility serves as a reminder that true greatness lies in kindness, wisdom, and the quiet strength of character.

Fostering Community and Belonging

Hanuman's journey was not a solitary endeavor; it was deeply rooted in the communities he served and the relationships he built. His actions reinforced the value of community, cooperation, and the strength found in unity. In our increasingly fragmented world, Hanuman's example prompts us to seek connection, to support one another, and to recognize that our collective well-being is intertwined with the well-being of others.

Cultivating Faith and Perseverance

Perhaps one of the most profound lessons from Hanuman's story is the power of faith—not just in the divine but in oneself. His perseverance, driven by faith in Lord Rama's righteousness and in his own abilities, offers a powerful testament to the miracles that faith and determination can achieve. It teaches us to hold fast to our beliefs, to persevere through challenges, and to trust in the journey, even when the path is uncertain.

Conclusion

As we reflect on Hanuman's legacy, we find not just a mythological hero but a source of inspiration for our own lives. His qualities—devotion, strength, humility, wisdom, and faith—serve as guiding principles for personal growth and resilience. Hanuman's story, echoing through centuries, continues to offer hope, strength, and a path to transcendence, reminding us of the infinite potential that resides within each of us.

Learning the lessons from Hanuman's life, we are encouraged to face our challenges with courage, to serve with a selfless heart, and to cultivate a life of purpose and devotion. Hanuman remains a beacon of hope and strength, guiding us towards our highest selves and the realization of our deepest potentials.

Major Characters In The Ramayana

The Ramayana is one of the two major Sanskrit epics of ancient Indian literature, the other being the Mahabharata. It explores the life of Rama, the prince of Ayodhya, and includes a rich tapestry of characters each embodying various virtues and vices. Below is a brief overview of the major characters in the Ramayana:

1. Shri Ram: The protagonist of the Ramayana, Rama is the seventh avatar of the Hindu god Vishnu. He is celebrated for his adherence to dharma (righteousness) despite the trials and tribulations he faces, including his 14-year exile and the rescue of his wife Sita from the demon king Ravana.

2. Sita: Rama's devoted wife and the incarnation of Goddess Lakshmi. Sita is revered for her unwavering fidelity and virtue, even under the duress of her abduction by Ravana.

3. Lakshmana: Rama's younger brother, renowned for his loyalty and the sacrifices he makes to accompany Rama and Sita during their exile. His life is a testament to his devotion to his brother and his willingness to face hardship.

4. Hanuman: A devotee of Rama, Hanuman is a pivotal character known for his unparalleled devotion, strength, and bravery. His feats, including finding Sita in Lanka and bringing the mountain with the Sanjeevani herb to save Lakshmana, are legendary.

5. Ravana: The ten-headed king of Lanka and the main antagonist of the epic. His abduction of Sita and his eventual defeat by Rama are central to the narrative. Ravana is also a complex character, known for his devotion to Shiva, his scholarly knowledge, and his prowess as a ruler.

6. Bharata: Rama's younger brother, known for his profound love and respect for Rama. He rules Ayodhya as Rama's proxy during his exile and is celebrated for his unwavering commitment to righteousness and duty.

7. Shatrughna: The youngest brother of Rama, known primarily for his companionship with Bharata and his participation in the campaign against the demon Lavana.

8. Dasharatha: The king of Ayodhya and father of Rama, Lakshmana, Bharata, and Shatrughna. His decision to send Rama into exile, prompted by a promise to his wife Kaikeyi, sets the stage for the epic's events.

9. Kaikeyi: The third wife of King Dasharatha, whose demand for Rama's exile and Bharata's enthronement arises from a desire to see her son as king, influenced by her maid Manthara.

10. Vibhishana: Ravana's brother, who, due to his righteousness, sides with Rama in the battle against Ravana. He is later crowned king of Lanka after Ravana's death.

11. Jatayu: A divine bird who attempts to rescue Sita from Ravana during her abduction. Although he fails and loses his life, his efforts are crucial in informing Rama and Lakshmana of Sita's abduction.

12. Valmiki: The author of the Ramayana and a sage who provides refuge to Sita after she is banished from Ayodhya. He is also the mentor to Sita's sons, Lava and Kusha.

These characters, with their distinct virtues and flaws, bring to life the rich narrative of the Ramayana, making it a timeless epic that explores the complexities of duty, righteousness, loyalty, and the struggles of divine and human natures.

References And Further Reading

For those inspired by the lessons and stories of Hanuman and the Ramayana, delving deeper into these subjects can enrich understanding and appreciation. Here are recommended resources for further exploration, ranging from ancient texts to contemporary analyses:

1. Primary Texts

The Ramayana: Multiple translations and adaptations of the Ramayana exist, offering various perspectives on the epic. Notable translations include those by R.K. Narayan, Valmiki (translated by Ralph T.H. Griffith), and Tulsidas' Ramcharitmanas (a version written in Awadhi).

Hanuman Chalisa: This devotional hymn by Tulsidas is available in various translations and commentaries, providing insights into its profound meanings.

2. Scholarly Analyses

"Hanuman: The Devotion and Power of the Monkey God" by Vanamali provides an in-depth look at Hanuman's role in Hindu mythology and his significance as a divine figure.

3. Cultural Studies

"Many Ramayanas: The Diversity of a Narrative Tradition in South Asia" edited by Paula Richman provides an exploration of the Ramayana's various tellings across different cultures and periods, highlighting the epic's broad impact and interpretations.

"Hanuman's Tale: The Messages of a Divine Monkey" by Philip Lutgendorf examines the cultural significance of Hanuman through history, literature, and religious practice.

4. Personal Growth and Spirituality

"Journey with Hanuman" by Swami Tejomayananda offers spiritual lessons drawn from Hanuman's qualities and deeds, applicable to personal development.

"Living Fearlessly: Bringing Out Your Inner Soul Strength" by Paramahansa Yogananda includes teachings and practices for overcoming fear and building inner strength, with references to Hanuman's example.

5. Online Resources

Various online platforms and websites provide access to lectures, courses, and discussions on the Ramayana and Hanuman. Websites like the Vedanta Society, ISKCON, and others offer spiritual interpretations and teachings based on these texts.

6. Multimedia

Documentaries, films, and animated stories about Hanuman and the Ramayana offer visual and engaging ways to explore the epic and its characters. YouTube and streaming services are good platforms to find such content.

When exploring these resources, consider the context in

which they were created and the perspectives they represent. Each interpretation of Hanuman's story and the Ramayana adds layers of meaning to the epic's rich tapestry, offering insights into its enduring relevance and power.